Unveiling Prosperity

Achieve a life of material and spiritual abundance.

INSIGHT

OF

PROSPERITY

Vol 1

By Sheka Mansaray

Revelation Publishing

Kingdom Revelation fit to print

DEDICATION

This book is dedicated to my Daughter Faith & My Son Sheka Jr who has been an inspiration to me to be able to do what is needed and set a stage for them to walk in their prosperous life.

**Save now, I beseech thee, O LORD: O LORD, I beseech
thee, send now prosperity.
Psalm 118:25**

Table of contents.

1. Introduction---pg 6
2. Definition of Prosperity--- pg 8
3. Old Testament Prosperity--- pg16
4. The Tithe under the Law---pg 20
5. Tithing for the New Testament---pg 22
6. Great Success Story ---pg 25
7. The Secrets of Abraham's Prosperity ---pg31
8. The Law to Seek many Happiness---pg 35
9. The Insight of Prosperity--- pg 41
10. To Be Rich--- pg45

Introduction

The purpose of this book is to remind you of what you may already know: that prosperity is your heritage. Every normal person is vitally interested in the subject of prosperity. *God wants you to prosper.* It is a fact of the gospel that Christians both overlook and grossly misunderstand. Though some false teachers would seek to preach a gospel that attempts to defraud people of true biblical prosperity through greed, self-centeredness, and Scripture-twisting, God has spelled out through the pages of Scripture exactly how he wants you to prosper. The way to enduring prosperity begins with a true love for God and obedience to what He commands through Scripture.

Prosperity is simply another word for well-being, often financial but also including health, happiness, or spiritual well-being. Of course, people think of prosperity in different ways so it can be hard to nail down a specific definition that makes everyone happy. It could be thought of generally as the absence of poverty, unhappiness, sickness, fear, and adversity. Material prosperity is an important part of the gospel message, but it is not the goal. The goal of the gospel is to reconcile man to God through Christ Jesus. For those who make the kingdom and Christ the focus of their life on earth, prosperity awaits.

Indeed, an expanded prosperity consciousness is a necessity in the age of increasing economic demands. Rising prices, inflationary recessions," and uncertain political and economic world conditions are all indications that we must raise and expand our consciousness to a new level of universal supply. Through using the prosperity laws described in this book, you can deliberately get into a universal prosperity vibration, and begin to experience more successful results in every phase of your life.

When you see the title of this lesson, I am sure that a lot of things run through your mind. Hopefully, you do not simply think about money even though money is certainly included in the subject of prosperity. Real prosperity involves life in my spirit, soul and body. A healthy spirit that is tuned to God and hears His voice is certainly biblical prosperity. A soul that has a renewed mind, emotions that are expressive about the Lord and a will that is submitted to God is certainly biblical prosperity. A body that is free of disease and has the works of the flesh crucified is certainly biblical prosperity. Circumstances that are under the dominion of the kingdom of God with a manifestation of finances to be a blessing to all around us is certainly biblical prosperity. You put all of these together and we are starting to see the heart of God in manifestation.

So with that being said I welcome you to a new Life of Prosperity God bless you.

Definition of Prosperity

A good definition of prosperity is the ability to call on the ability of God to meet the need of mankind. If I am prosperous, then I can go to my loving Father and receive the wisdom and understanding to accomplish anything that the world or the enemy of my soul might bring my way. If it turns out that finances are needed, the Lord will then show me how to prosper (Isaiah 48:17). If healing is what I need, the Spirit of God is in me to quicken and make alive my mortal body. Whatever the need, I can be taught the ways of God which will cause me to prosper. Prosperity means to succeed, to flourish, to thrive, and to have economic success.

Even though finances are just a small part of prosperity, we want to focus on money during this lesson. I want to emphasize this is not a pursuit of things; it is about the pursuit of God. Only when we pursue the Lord will "all" the things we need be ours. The good news is that Jesus showed us how to walk in mastery over finances in order that I could be shown how to handle the true riches as well as an abundance of natural riches. Matthew 19:16-30 explains a case study of the Lord and the rich young man with social status. The young man was confident that he could keep all the Law and was doing precisely just that. Jesus knows our heart and the area of weakness in our flesh. Jesus confronted him in his weakness with a loving heart so that the young man could be healed and continue his way healed and mature.

Jesus suggested that he love his neighbor in a tangible way and give them all his belongings. He went away mad because his heart was truly shown. The young man had a heart full of the love of money, not a heart of compassion like his Heavenly Father. The young man did not understand that he did not own the finances. Just because he received the riches by work or inheritance does not mean they were his. We know that everything is the Lord's and He lets us be a steward over His riches. As a steward, the rich young man had an opportunity to act on Proverbs 19:17 and watch the blessings of the Law overtake him. Jesus was not trying to make the young man poor, but rich towards God. When we are rich toward God, we will begin to enjoy true prosperity in all areas of our lives. Jesus was teaching about getting our heart focused correctly so our treasures will be stored in the right place. (Matthew 6:21)

As we look at the Kingdom Way of doing things, we quickly realize that the wisdom of God is necessary if we are to walk in the prosperity that He has for us. The Lord's heart is prosperity in every aspect of our lives. Isaiah 48:17 states that the Lord will teach us how to prosper and Deuteronomy 8:18 explains that He will give us the ability to prosper and gain wealth. Proverbs 3:13-18 amplifies the heart of God when Solomon states the wisdom of the Lord gives us greater consequences than gold. Gold would certainly be a blessing in my life, but the word says that God's wisdom is even greater and will have far more reaching benefits. The word becomes a fountain of blessing.

In Acts 18 we see Paul working with Aquila making tents to support himself and the ministry, but in Acts 19:1 we see Paul traveling and not having to make tents because others were supporting the ministry. Paul was prosperous in both places because he was being obedient to God. My bank account is not the measure of my success, but my willingness and obedience to do the will of God is my place of prosperity. Money should not dictate whether I can do the will of God. The Lord's plans give me a future and a hope (Jeremiah 29:11) not my bank account. Finances are necessary for the full plan the Lord has for me. II Corinthians 9:8 says that I should be able to liberally give into all good works as well as being able to respond to the Lord's voice no matter what the financial requirement might be. III John 1:6 shows us that people should be able to help finance those in the traveling ministry in a worthy manner. Abraham, David, Solomon and many others in the bible lived in such a way that they could be a blessing financially to those around them. Romans 12:8 shows us how that Father gives some people the ability to move in an extraordinary way in the realm of finances. If being wealthy was wrong, then God Himself would be in error, because He is wealthy as well as giving many others this ability to imitate Him in this area. None of us would ever make the statement that God's prosperity is wrong, but we do sometimes criticize His sons and daughters that have been blessed financially. Keep remembering that the Lord is looking for stewards that will take from His provision and give to His people. (I Corinthians 4:1,2).

Living in financial abundance is a journey. I am sure you are progressing in your understanding of the Lord's financial plan and His way of handling money. III John 1:2 is certainly a key to moving in abundance as well as Joshua 1:8. Both scriptures show us that the way to reach the height of prosperity that the Lord has for me is to begin the journey with a determination to meditate and act on His word. We start by seeking the Lord and we will reach the end by seeking the Lord. As we journey through the Lord's Word, allow the Word to teach you to prosper and show you your point of obedience.

Definitions: Prosper: (Hebrew) Tsaleach. Be profitable, break out, be good, make prosperous, to accomplish, finish, complete and succeed. Causing a journey to prosper or succeed and reach its goal or purpose.

Prosper: (Hebrew) Osher. To accumulate.

Prosper: (Hebrew) Cheyil. Wealth, substance, power, strength, army, to prosper, be firm, be strong, be mighty, and be enduring.

Prosper: (Hebrew) Hown. Wealth, riches, substance, enough

Prosper: (Greek) Euodoo.To be on a right road, unhindered journey, to be successfully reach the destination safe and sound, receiving help and being on a road that is easy to travel, and a blessing.

Prosper: (English) To succeed, to flourish, to thrive and to have economic success.

Scripture Application:

1. Genesis 2:8-17

2. Genesis 8:22

3. Genesis 9:27

4. Genesis 14:17-24

5. Genesis 15:1-6

6. Genesis 15:8-21

7. Genesis 17:1,2

8. Genesis 21:1-7

9. Genesis 22:14

10. Genesis 24:6-9

11. Genesis 24:34-41

12. Genesis 24:59,60

13. Genesis 26: 3-6

14. Genesis 26: 12-18

15. Genesis 28: 3,14,15

16. Genesis 30:28-33

17. Genesis 31:41,42

18. Genesis 33:9

19. Genesis 39:3-5,9

20. Genesis 39:20-23

Is it the will of God for His people to have material prosperity in this world? Is it in accordance with His plan that they have large possessions of this world's goods? These have long been muted and controversial questions. In fact, there are few questions as important that have been left as open as these. Today, there are deep searching's of the heart among many of God's people for the real truth of the matter. There are some who would teach that poverty is a blessing. They point out that the disciples who followed Jesus were poor, and at times did not have money to pay a simple tax.

They also note that many of the great saints during this age have suffered poverty and hardship. They contend that God's blessing has been upon the poor rather than upon those who have possession of unusual amounts of this world's goods. They point out, moreover, that many of the characters of Old Testament times served the Lord faithfully until they had achieved prosperity, and then they failed God. However, while it is true that riches have often resulted in people becoming proud and arrogant, yet it is also common knowledge that the poor can be just as deficient in character as the rich. It is a matter of record that out of poverty have arisen many great men. But there have been godly men of wealth also—such as Abraham. It is yet to be proved that either poverty or riches, in themselves, are the final answer to the problem of developing Christian character. But one thing is certain: the right use of wealth is of the utmost importance in the determining of human destiny. Much has been written about tithing being the key to prosperity. We believe the Bible bears out that the teaching of tithing is sound and scriptural; in this book, I have taken consideration of this truth. However, we must add that it is our belief that in general writers have stopped short of the full answer to the question of Christian prosperity. Jesus plainly told of a master key to material blessings in this world.

Strangely enough, little has been said or written about this keys. Yet just as tithing was the master key in the Old Testament to temporal blessing (and is still important in the New), so there is prosperity in the New Testament. One thing we should note. Although Jesus spoke again and again against covetousness, which is the desire for wealth for the purpose of hoarding it, He never said that Christians should avoid material possessions, nor that they should seek poverty for poverty's sake. He did say, "But seek ye first the kingdom of God, and his righteousness; and all these things shall be added unto you" (Matt. 6:33). Jesus taught that first and foremost, it is the responsibility of every human being to seek the kingdom of God. He said, "No man can serve two masters... Ye cannot serve God and mammon" (Matt. 6:24). Nevertheless, the thought is clearly expressed by Jesus that if a man puts God first, then God will put him first. If a man truly seeks the kingdom of God he need not be anxious about the material things of life. God will meet his needs and give him an abundance of material blessings in due time. As John the beloved wrote in his last epistle: "Beloved, I wish above all things that thou mayest prosper and be in health, even as thy soul prospereth" (III John 2).

What then is this unveiling prosperity? Of that we shall take due note in this book. Opening of the book God wants His people to be prosperous, which includes finances, good health, good marriages and relationships, i.e...I looked around upon the world, and saw that it was shadowed by sorrow and scorched by the fierce fires of suffering. And I looked for the cause. I looked around, but could not find it; I looked in books, but could not find it; I looked within, and found there both the cause and the self-made nature of that cause. I looked again, and deeper, and found the remedy. I found one Law, the Law of Love; one Life, the Life of adjustment to that Law; one Truth, the truth of a conquered mind and a quiet and obedient heart. And I dreamed of writing a book which should help men and women, whether rich or poor, learned or unlearned, worldly or unworldly, to find within themselves the source of all success, all happiness, all accomplishment, all truth. And the dream remained with me, and at last became substantial; and now I send it forth into the world on its mission of healing and blessedness, knowing that it cannot fail to reach the homes and hearts of those who are waiting and ready to receive it.

Old Testament Prosperity

The first words of the Bible are, "In the beginning God created the heaven and the earth" (Gen. 1:1). Therefore, creation belongs to Him and He has the right to ordain the laws by which it is governed, After ordering the earth and providing the conditions that would make it a home for mankind, God created Adam and Eve and made them progenitors of the human race. THE GARDEN OF EDEN (Gen. 2, 3) Now the first words which God spoke to man have vital significance to our subject: the law of prosperity. God said: "Of every tree of the garden thou mayest freely eat: But of the tree of the knowledge of good and evil, thou shalt not eat of it: for in the day that thou eatest thereof thou shalt surely die" (Gen. 2:16, 17). Here God stated a great principle. He had placed man in the Garden of the Lord and had provided every blessing for his happiness and pleasure.

Nothing was required to obtain any of these blessings, temporal or otherwise. All had been freely provided. With one notable exception, it was Adam and Eve's privilege to partake of any tree of the Garden. However, and this was important, there was one tree God had reserved for Himself, and man was to leave it strictly alone—that was the tree of knowledge of good and evil. Now it was in man's hand to either respect this commandment, or to disobey it. But because the fruit of the tree appeared to be good for food, and desirable to make one wise,

Adam and Eve chose to accept Satan's lie and disbelieve God. They reached forth their hand and the irrevocable deed was done. The tragic result that followed their fateful act need not be elaborated on. The curse came upon them swiftly and surely. A train of sin, evil, pain, sorrow, sickness and death followed their trail and that of their descendants—a trail of misery and woe that still continues. God had given man every blessing he needed, but had reserved something for Himself. Man violated this law, took what belonged to God, and the curse came upon him. Driven from Eden he had to earn his living by the sweat of his brow. The ground violated the law of prosperity, and now became subject to the law of poverty and death. The fact is that God, in giving His blessings to man, always reserves something for Himself which He requires to be kept inviolate. This brings us to the law of the tithe which is one of the vital keys to the enjoyment of temporal prosperity.

ABRAHAM AND THE TITHE (Gen. 14: 18-24) The Bible in a few brief chapters relates the events of the first two thousand years of human history. But with the appearance of Abraham (whose experiences we have already recorded) the biblical narrative goes into detail of God's dealings with man. After a sad story of self-will that dominates the scene in both pre and postdiluvian days, there appears this man Abraham who will listen to the voice of God—a man who believed in giving to God what belonged to Him, and who recognized that God was the author of all true prosperity. In the previous chapter we discussed six of the great rules of prosperity which were demonstrated in the life of Abraham, and noted also that there was a seventh. Because this seventh rule is the keystone to the Old Testament plan of prosperity, we deferred discussion of it to this present chapter. What was this Old Testament key to temporal prosperity? The answer is one that all of us should know. It is the law of the tithe, which involves the tenth of our increase.

Abraham learned that there was a direct relation between giving the tithe and the enjoyment of temporal prosperity. He recognized and acknowledged that in a peculiar way, one tenth of all he possessed belonged to God, and he was always careful to see that it got into God's hands. The tithe was instituted for a purpose. Even in that day God had a priesthood to be supported. There was Melchizedek, king of Salem, priest of the most high God. While the kings of the surrounding nations were fighting over possession of the earth, Abraham took time to see that God's ministry was taken care of. Fresh from the battle in which he had defeated Tidal king of nations, Abraham went to the residence of Melchizedek king of Salem, and "gave him tithes of all." "And Melchizedek king of Salem brought forth bread and wine: and he was the priest of the most high God. And he blessed him, and said, Blessed be Abram of the most high God, possessor of heaven and earth: And blessed be the most high God, which hath delivered thine enemies into thy hand. And he gave him tithes of all" (Gen. 14:18-20). It was the law of the tithe. Abraham obeyed the law of the tithe and God prospered him. While the kings and princes were seeking wealth by taking it by force, while the inhabitants of Sodom thought they could prosper as they multiplied wickedness, while Lot chose to sit in the gate of Sodom and become a great man in this world, Abraham remembered the law of prosperity and fulfilled his obligation in payment of the tithe. And Abraham prospered and enjoyed riches, temporal and spiritual, for three-quarters of a century after Sodom and Gomorrah had been reduced to ashes! "And Abram was very rich in cattle, in silver, and in gold" (Gen. 13:2). "And the Lord hath blessed my master greatly; and he is become great: and he hath given him flocks, and herds and silver, and gold, and menservants, and maidservants, and camels, and asses" (Gen. 24:35).

JACOB AND HIS PROMISE TO GOD (Gen. 28) We have noted how Jacob had sought the birthright and the blessing, and had taken them by craft and sharp bargaining. But he was to learn that no one steals the blessings of heaven, or at least keeps them, who doesn't play the game according to the rules. All his scheming had gone for naught. He had incurred the hatred of his twin brother, Esau, and was forced to flee for his life. No doubt realizing his folly, and knowing that he would perhaps never see his mother's face again, Jacob did some serious thinking. As night drew on, he stopped at Bethel and laid his head upon a stone that he had set up for a pillow. That night Jacob had his first spiritual experience. During his troubled sleep he had a vision of angels ascending and descending a ladder reaching up to heaven. It was here that he met God for the first time. In the morning, he took the stone that he had laid under his head and anointed it. And there he made his covenant with God. It is at Bethel that we have the first Bible recorded instance of conversion.

It was the conversion of a man who had gotten into trouble. Jacob hardly knew where his next meal was coming from. Would he perish from hunger? Who would clothe him? The precariousness of his situation was very real. But that morning Jacob made a covenant to serve God. Knowing that his grandfather, Abraham, and no doubt his father, Isaac, had paid tithes, he now made the vow to do likewise. And here was the vow that Jacob made: "And Jacob vowed a vow, saying, If God will be with me, and will keep me in this way that I go, and will give me bread to eat, and raiment to put on, So that I come again to my father's house in peace; then shall the Lord be my God: And this stone, which I have set for a pillar, shall be God's house: and of all that thou shalt give me I will surely give the tenth unto thee" (Genesis 28:20-22). Jacob never wanted for bread or for raiment, although he came close to it many times. Actually for his duplicity and trickery he deserved to starve, yet God in His mercy was with him. Though He had to chasten Jacob and though for many years the man was to reap the results of his misdeeds, God took him through all the way. And the time did come when his trials and tribulations ended. The closing years of his life were blessed indeed. Joseph, his son, brought him down to Egypt to share in his glory and great prosperity.

THE TITHE UNDER THE LAW

(Lev. 27:30-31) The tithe was given under the Law but as we have seen, the tithe did not originate under the Law. It was in existence in the days of Abraham and Jacob and no doubt long before. The tithe was the law of God and therefore with the giving of the Mosaic Law it was only natural that this should be incorporated in it. (Even as for example the law of the sanctity of human life, instituted long before the Law, was included in it Gen. 9:6 and Exod. 20:13.) And so it was when the Law was given, the commandment concerning the law of the tithe was expressly stated. The tithe or one-tenth was God's to take care of His work. "And all the tithe of the land, whether of the seed of the land, or of the fruit of the tree, is the Lord's: it is holy unto the Lord. And if a man will at all redeem ought of his tithes, he shall add thereto the fifth part thereof" (Lev. 27:30, 31). Here is an interesting note: The question is raised as to whether in an emergency one might temporarily borrow part of the tithe.

God knew that people, in the midst of financial pressure, would be under temptation to use a part of their tithe, no doubt with good intentions of replacing it later. He knew that in so doing people would find it difficult in many cases to repay what they had borrowed. It was therefore not a good practice. So although God did not forbid borrowing of the tithe, He did set up a safeguard to discourage the practice. If the tithe were borrowed to take care of an emergency, the borrower was not only to repay it, but to add a fifth thereto! That is twenty percent. Rather high interest! True, but God did not want people appropriating the tithe and then finding themselves when they could not pay it back. He did not want them to bring themselves under the curse which would come if they misappropriated God's money. The fact that God charged interest for the use of the tithe dramatically demonstrates that He considers the tithe as His exclusively. Why did God regard the tithe as so important? First, the tithe made possible the support of His ministry. And second, the tithe was the key feature in His plan for giving financial security to His people. The tithe could be compared as it were to the premium of an insurance policy. Failure to keep up the premium would cause the policy to lapse. Likewise failure to be scrupulous in the payment of the tithe cancelled God's obligation to provide financial security for the defaulter.

Tithing for the New Testament

There yet remains an important question to answer. Is tithing for the New Testament age? This question failed to have significance in the Early Church for one very good reason. The people sold all they had and brought the money and laid it at the apostles' feet! They gave all. During those days they lived in communal style and had all things common. Ordinarily, during the church age, this method has not been found practical. People live better in families than in communals, a system that Communism makes work at the point of a gun. But Christians do not use guns in spreading the Gospel. Communals are not a sound plan for ordinary living. They are for emergencies. People may live together satisfactorily in large numbers during a flood, a disaster, or during a war that sweeps through their land. But after the emergency is over they desire to return to their homes. In the Early Church there was an emergency.

The new Christians were in danger of their lives. A relentless persecution by the Jewish hierarchy kept the infant church in a constant state of jeopardy. The people were glad to live together and enjoy the mutual security that was thus provided. They sold all they had and laid it at the feet of the apostles. However, the time came when circumstances changed and the communal system was abandoned. For the above reason, tithing was not practiced during the first few years of the Early Church—simply because the people did not have their separate homes, and they gave all that they had to the church. However, the Scriptures, recognizing that this change would come, and that the communal system was not permanent, plainly taught that tithing was also God's plan during the New Testament age. In these events that took place in the days of the Early Church we find that people, in going beyond the law of the tithe, were discovering the New Testament key to absolute security and the best that God has.

JESUS SAID MEN OUGHT TO TITHE Jesus spoke on the subject of tithing. He indeed showed that it was not enough to tithe and to omit "judgment, mercy and faith." Just the act of tithing cannot atone for other serious omissions. So that He would not be misunderstood, Jesus commended the fact of tithing but told the Pharisees that they ought to do the other also. "Ye pay tithe of mint and anise and cummin, and have omitted the weightier matters of the law, judgment, mercy, and faith: these ought ye to have done, and not to leave the other undone" (Matt. 23:23). The point we are concerned with here is: Jesus taught that men ought to pay tithes. So far as we know the Pharisees, who tithed, enjoyed material prosperity, although they suffered spiritual loss because of their blindness and inability to recognize the "day of their visitation." Note this: The Lord commended tithing, but showed that there was something more. That there is something more is a hint that beyond the act of tithing God has a master key for Christian prosperity.

TITHING IN THE NEW TESTAMENT CHURCH

There are some who insist that tithing has no force in the New Testament Church, and that it is only a part of the Mosaic Law. In this, however, they are mistaken. Tithing was instituted long before the Law. Both Abraham and Jacob paid tithes. It is true that tithing, as well as other obligations, is considered in the New Testament as a privilege rather than a command. Believers should do things because they love the Lord rather than because they are forced to do them. Nevertheless, the laws governing prosperity are just as cogent in the New Testament as in the Old. And certainly, if we receive more under grace than under the Law, we should feel as responsible to do as much, if not more, than those who lived under the Old Testament. Nevertheless, that there be no mistake, the Scriptures clearly show that tithing was practiced by the New Testament Church. This is plainly spoken of in Heb. 7:8: "And here men that die receive tithes; but there he receiveth them, of whom it is witnessed that he liveth." Note the book of Hebrews was written some 35 years after the institution of the church. The inspired writer says, "Here men that die receive tithes; but there he receiveth them, of whom it is witnessed that he liveth." Thirtyfive years passed and ministers still received tithes! But who were those ministers? Is the Scripture here referring to the apostate Jewish religionists who had rejected Christ? Is this tithing that of the followers of the Pharisees who put Christ to death and who attempted to stamp out Christianity? Of course not. Christ Himself is spoken of as receiving the tithes.

Money given to the Christ-rejecting Jewish hierarchy could not be said to be received by the Lord. Only that which was given to His ministers could be accepted by Him. And here is a striking truth. Those who tithe may seem to be giving to man, but indeed their tithes are actually being received and accepted by Christ! They are received by the One "who dieth no more," but lives for evermore! Thirty-five years after Christ ascended to heaven, acting in His high priesthood after the order of Melchizedek, He received tithes from men. And He still does! How important it is then that as stewards we see that which belongs to Christ is given unto Him. We do not in truth give them to men. Actually the minister is only another steward to whom we give our tithes. They are received by Christ to whom they belong!

GIVING TO CHRIST FOR MISSIONS

There is the story of a missionary who had returned to his home city, where he announced a collection for foreign missions. A good friend said to him: "Very well, sheka, seeing it's for you, I'll give 100 marks." "No," said the missionary, "I cannot take the money since you give it seeing me." The man saw the point and said: "You are right, Sheka. Here are 200 marks, seeing it's for the Lord Jesus." The missionary was right. If the man was to get a blessing out of his giving, he must see Christ as he gave. And how differently we give when we realize that we are indeed giving to Christ.

Great Success Story

As an introduction to this book prosperity, we shall consider the story of two great Bible characters. The lives of these two men illustrate the working of this divine law of temporal prosperity—how that heeding it brought good success to one, while failure and trouble came to the other who disregarded it. With the first of these two, the pursuit of wealth had actually little or no place. Nevertheless he became a rich man. Not only did he gain great wealth, but God gave him many years to enjoy his prosperity. The other man also had faith, although his faith was of a mixed kind. He believed in God, desired His blessings, but at the same time was possessed of a driving ambition to become rich, an ambition he would gratify, if necessary, at the expense of others. The methods that he employed to achieve success have ever since been a classic example of the wrong way to get rich. He did, however, finally learn his lesson, and from that time sought to walk the life of a true pilgrim. God brought him eventually into a place of peace, and during the sunset of his life Jacob enjoyed the blessings of prosperity and of a united family. God has given us the stories of these two men as examples of the right way and the wrong way to achieve prosperity.

ABRAHAM—FATHER OF THE FAITHFUL Abraham is indeed a unique Bible character, in that to an almost equal degree he enjoyed both great spiritual and temporal blessings. He was rich in silver and gold; he was also rich in his knowledge and understanding of Jehovah. As a reward for his consecration and obedience, God gave promises to Abraham that He gave to no one else. Abraham was to become father of the faithful. Kings were to come from his loins. His seed was to become as the sands of the sea and the stars of the heavens for multitude. He was not only to be blessed, but his obedience was to reach out and bless generations in all ages to come. Let us now seek to discover the secret that made this man's success so great.

ABRAHAM LEFT ALL TO OBEY GOD. (Gen. 12) When God called Abraham, He did not promise him that He was going to prosper his business or show him the way to make a fortune. Instead, God called him to leave all! "Get thee out of thy country, and from thy kindred and from thy father's house, unto a land that I will show thee" (Gen. 12:1). Had Abraham had his eye on becoming wealthy he would no doubt have remained in Haran. Encyclopedia Americana says, "Haran...to the Assyrians was a strategic post of great importance. An extensive commerce centered there." Apparently Abraham's father, Terah, had accumulated property in Haran. Abraham would have had to remain there to have inherited this property. But God called the patriarch to journey to a land that he had never seen and there to begin a new life.

Abraham was more interested in God's inheritance than in that of his father, Terah, who lived in a land of idolatry (Joshua 24:14-15). He was concerned more with that city "whose builder and maker is God" (Heb. 11:10). He made the decision to put God first in everything. And that resolution guided every decision he would make in the future. And so Abraham, disregarding his prospects in Haran, journeyed on to the land of Canaan. But did Abraham find things inviting when he reached that land? Hardly! He got there at just the time of a great famine! It looked very much as if he had made the greatest mistake of his life. Abraham and his household were scarcely able to find enough to eat. Under pressure of the famine, he journeyed down into Egypt, a place where he soon ran into more difficulties. Everything seemed to go wrong. It must have appeared to those of his company that Abraham had made a serious mistake.

Nevertheless, the prophet, neither then nor later, ever allowed himself to doubt God. For him there was no turning back. He had burned the bridges behind him, and he had no intention of returning to Haran. God had told him He would bless and prosper him. Somehow he believed that God's promise would be fulfilled.

ABRAHAM WAS NOTED FOR HIS GENEROSITY
(Gen: 13, 14)

Now Abraham had brought his nephew, Lot, along with him. After Abraham had returned to Canaan, following the famine referred to, he enjoyed a period of real prosperity. His flocks and herds and those of his nephew, Lot, multiplied to such numbers that there was not room for them all to dwell together. At this point in their sojourning, they had come to the borders of a valley in the plain of the Jordan. Although this area around Sodom and Gomorrah was soon to come under divine judgment it was nevertheless at that time "as the garden of the Lord" (Gen. 13:10). It must have seemed a tempting place for Abraham to settle down and make his home. As chieftain of his company, he had the right of first choice. But Abraham saw that Lot desired it and he let him have what he wanted. He himself took the land which his nephew evidently thought was a much less favorable choice than the valley. But neither Abraham nor Lot had any anticipation that even then, the cities of the plains were about to come under divine judgment. For a time Lot prospered in the plains of Sodom; but one day a war broke out. Some tribal kings came against Sodom because that city had decided it would no longer pay tribute. In the battle, the king of Sodom and his confederate kings were defeated. The invaders gathered up the wealth of the cities that could be carried away and took the inhabitants, including the family of Lot, into captivity— presumably to become slaves. Abraham mobilized his company and pursued them. In the darkness they made a surprise attack, defeating the host of the enemy and recovering the hostages as well as the goods that had been taken. The king of Sodom offered to make a deal.

If Abraham would return the captives he could keep the goods. But Abraham's answer was: "I will not take from a thread even to a shoe latchet, and that I will not take any thing that is thine, lest thou shouldest say, I have made Abram rich" (Gen. 14:23). If God was going to prosper Abraham, He must do it in His own way. Abraham would not have it said that the king of Sodom had made him rich. He knew the exceeding wickedness of that city. Apparently he wanted to have nothing to do with those who lived in those cities. He did not want to be linked up or associated with the king of Sodom in any way. Abraham was a generous man and given to hospitality, as shown on the occasion when he "entertained angels unawares" (Heb. 13:2 and Gen. 18). He did not gain his wealth by shrewd dealing, by driving sharp bargains with his fellowmen, or by exploiting his office as a prophet. When Abraham sought a burial place for his wife, Sarah, he refused the offer of the children of Heth to accept a plot of ground without cost. Abraham knew that the gift was given merely because he was reckoned as a great man (Gen. 23:6). The world always considers it politic to give gifts to important men. Abraham refused the gift, even as he refused everything that belonged to the king of Sodom.

ABRAHAM'S SUPREME TEST (Gen. 22) But Abraham's great and supreme test came when he was asked to offer up his only son Isaac as a sacrifice. Would even Abraham be able to face and pass such a supreme test of his faith in God? Many would like to share the blessings of Abraham, but would they be willing to pass through the same tests? In observing Abraham's complete surrender to the absolute will of God we shall find the key to the mighty blessings that he received. The incident of the offering of Isaac has long been one over which the critics have stumbled. We shall briefly take note of this before we consider the lesson that it teaches. The critics' objection is that the incident supposedly teaches the offering of human sacrifice. Actually, as we shall see, it teaches the very opposite! First, as all Bible readers know, the incident typifies the offering of Christ by the Father for the sins of the world. Abraham in his role as father of Isaac was a type of the Father who "spared not his own Son, but delivered him up for us all" (Rom. 8:32), and Isaac was a type of Christ who was "obedient unto death" (Phil. 2:5-8). Second, Isaac, in another way, typifies the fallen human race, which in view of divine justice is doomed to die. However, mercy prevailed over justice by providing a substitutionary sacrifice in Christ, of which the ram caught in the thicket is the type. Concerning this supposed objection that the story teaches human sacrifice: actually, the whole incident was God's protest against that heathen custom! In the days of Abraham this cruel practice was widespread. It was extensively practiced by many Canaanite tribes at that time, as the research of modern archeology shows. Abraham was familiar with this heathen ritual and knew that its practice was widespread. He was deeply grieved when God proposed that he offer up Isaac, his son.

Yet so deep was his consecration to the will of God that he did not reason nor hesitate to obey what he knew was the voice of God. But although Abraham did not know it, God had no intention of having Isaac offered up as a human sacrifice. At the last moment the angel of the Lord appeared and directed Abraham's attention to the ram which was to take Isaac's place. Far from teaching human sacrifice, God was taking this occasion to show for all time to come that the practice is wrong and wholly unnecessary. God has provided a substitute sacrifice in Christ, and therefore human beings are never to be so offered. Indeed, such a sacrifice, great as it would cost a parent, could accomplish nothing. Abraham met the supreme test and passed it with flying colors. He had truly shown that he was willing if need to be to give up all to God, retaining nothing. Because he had withheld nothing, he now became the recipient of the greatest blessing that God could give any man. "And he said. Lay not thine hand upon the lad, neither do thou anything unto him: for now I know that thou fearest God, seeing thou hast not withheld thy son, thine only son from me... By myself have I sworn, saith the Lord, for because thou hast done this thing, and hast not withheld thy son, thine only son: That in blessing I will bless thee, and in multiplying I will multiply thy seed as the stars of the heaven, and as the sand which is upon the sea shore; and thy seed shall possess the gate of his enemies; And in thy seed shall all the nations of the earth be blessed; because thou hast obeyed my voice" (Gen. 22:12, 16- 18). Because Abraham was obedient, God promised him the very gates of the earth, and that his seed would be as the stars of heaven in multitude. Abraham, by giving all, had thus gained all. By leaving all, he had obtained all. By seeking spiritual things he received temporal things also. Here was a man who had learned the secret of receiving both spiritual and temporal blessings.

THE SECRETS OF ABRAHAM'S PROSPERITY

1. Abraham forsook all to obey God.

2. He refused to turn back in the midst of test.

3. He did not seek wealth by sharp practices.

4. He refused the wealth of Sodom (type of the world).

5. He was generous and honest.

6. He met the supreme test of obeying God if it cost him everything.

7. He obeyed the law of the tithe. Have you read the story of Abraham carefully? If so, you may have recognized in it the clue to the master key of an abundant prosperity.

Debt

- **Proverbs 22:7:** Just as the rich rule the poor, so the borrower is servant to the lender.
- **Romans 13:8:** Owe nothing to anyone—except for your obligation to love one another. If you love your neighbor, you will fulfill the requirements of God's law.

Financial Responsibility

- **1 Timothy 5:8:** But those who won't care for their relatives, especially those in their own household, have denied the true faith. Such people are worse than unbelievers.
- **Luke 16:11:** And if you are untrustworthy about worldly wealth, who will trust you with the true riches of heaven?
- **Proverbs 13:22:** Good people leave an inheritance to their grandchildren, but the sinner's wealth passes to the godly.
- **Proverbs 21:20:** The wise have wealth and luxury, but fools spend whatever they get.

Giving

- **Luke 6:38:** Give, and you will receive. Your gift will return to you in full—pressed down, shaken together to make room for more, running over, and poured into your lap. The amount you give will determine the amount you get back.
- **Proverbs 3:9-10:** Honor the Lord with your wealth and with the best part of everything you produce. Then he will fill your barns with grain, and your vats will overflow with good wine.
- **Malachi 3:8-10:** "Should people cheat God? Yet you have cheated me! "But you ask, 'What do you mean? When did we ever cheat you?' "You have cheated me of the tithes and offerings due to me. You are under a curse, for your whole nation has been cheating me. Bring all the tithes into the storehouse so there will be enough food in my

Temple. If you do," says the Lord of Heaven's Armies, "I will open the windows of heaven for you. I will pour out a blessing so great you won't have enough room to take it in! Try it! Put me to the test!"

- **Deuteronomy 16:17:** All must give as they are able, according to the blessings given to them by the Lord your God.
- **Luke 21:1-4:** While Jesus was in the Temple, he watched the rich people dropping their gifts in the collection box. Then a poor widow came by and dropped in two small coins. "I tell you the truth," Jesus said, "this poor widow has given more than all the rest of them. For they have given a tiny part of their surplus, but she, poor as she is, has given everything she has."

Greed

- **1 Timothy 6:10-11:** For the love of money is the root of all kinds of evil. And some people, craving money, have wandered from the true faith and pierced themselves with many sorrows. But you, Timothy, are a man of God; so run from all these evil things. Pursue righteousness and a godly life, along with faith, love, perseverance, and gentleness.
- **Hebrews 13:5:** Don't love money; be satisfied with what you have. For God has said, "I will never fail you. I will never abandon you."
- **Luke 12:15:** Then he said, "Beware! Guard against every kind of greed. Life is not measured by how much you own."

God's Provision

- **Philippians 4:19:** And this same God who takes care of me will supply all your needs from his glorious riches, which have been given to us in Christ Jesus.
- **Proverbs 10:22:** The blessing of the Lord makes a person rich, and he adds no sorrow with it.
- **2 Corinthians 9:8:** And God will generously provide all you need. Then you will always have everything you need and plenty left over to share with others.
- **Jeremiah 17:7-8:** But blessed are those who trust in the Lord and have made the Lord their hope and confidence. They are like trees planted along a riverbank, with roots that reach deep into the water. Such trees are not bothered by the heat or worried by long months of drought. Their leaves stay green, and they never stop producing fruit.

THE LAW TO SEEK MANY HAPPINESS

The law curves not for me, but I must bend unto the law, if I would reach the end of my afflictions, if I would restore My soul to Light and Life, and weep no more. Not mine the arrogant and selfish claim to all good things; be mine the lowly aim to seek and find, to know and comprehend, and wisdom-ward all holy footsteps wend, Nothing is mine to claim or to command, But all is mine to know and understand. Great is the thirst for happiness, and equally great is the lack of happiness.

The majority of the poor long for riches, believing that their possession would bring them supreme and lasting happiness. Many who are rich, having gratified every desire and whim, suffer from ennui and repletion, and are farther from the possession of happiness even than the very poor. If we reflect upon this state of things it will ultimately lead us to a knowledge of the all-important truth that happiness is not derived from mere outward possessions, nor misery from the lack of them; for if this were so, we should find the poor always miserable, and the rich always happy, whereas the reverse is frequently the case. Some of the most wretched people whom I have known while growing up in Sierra Leone are those who were surrounded with poverty, riches and luxury, whilst some of the brightest and happiest people I have met were possessed of only the barest necessities of life.

Many men who have accumulated riches have confessed that the selfish gratification which followed the acquisition of riches has robbed life of its sweetness, and that they were never so happy as when they were poor. What, then, is happiness, and how is it to be secured? Is it a figment, a delusion, and is suffering alone perennial? We shall find, after earnest observation and reflection, that all, except those who have entered the way of wisdom, believe that happiness is only to be obtained by the gratification of desire. It is this belief, rooted in the soil of ignorance, and continually watered by selfish cravings, that is the cause of all the misery in the world. And I do not limit the word desire to the grosser animal cravings; it extends to the higher psychic realm, where far more powerful, subtle, and insidious cravings hold in bondage the intellectual and refined, depriving them of all that beauty, harmony, and purity of soul whose expression is happiness.

Most people will admit that selfishness is the cause of all the unhappiness in the world, but they fall under the soul-destroying delusion that it is somebody else's selfishness, and not their own. When you are willing to admit that all your unhappiness is the result of your own selfishness you will not be far from the gates of Paradise; but so long as you are convinced that it is the selfishness of others that is robbing you of joy, so long will you remain a prisoner in your self-created agony. Happiness is that inward state of perfect satisfaction which is joy and peace, and from which all desire is eliminated. The satisfaction which results from gratified desire is brief and illusionary, and is always followed by an increased demand for gratification. Desire is as insatiable as the ocean, and clamors louder and louder as its demands are attended to. It claims ever-increasing service from its deluded devotees, until at last they are struck down with physical or mental anguish, and are hurled into the purifying fires of suffering. Desire is the region of hell, and all torments are centered there. The giving up of desire is the realization of heaven, and all delights await the pilgrim there, I sent my soul through the invisible, Some letter of that after life

pg. 37

to spell, And by-and-by my soul returned to me, And whispered, "I myself am heaven and hell,"

The Path of Prosperity, Heaven and hell are inward states. Sink into self and all its gratifications, and you sink into hell; rise above self into that state of consciousness which is the utter denial and forgetfulness of self, and you enter heaven. Self is blind, without judgment, not possessed of true knowledge, and always leads to suffering. Correct perception, unbiased judgment, and true knowledge belong only to the divine state, and only in so far as you realize this divine consciousness can you know what real happiness is. So long as you persist in selfishly seeking for your own personal happiness, so long will happiness elude you, and you will be sowing the seeds of wretchedness. In so far as you succeed in losing yourself in the service of others, in that measure will happiness come to you, and you will reap a harvest of bliss. It is in loving, not in being loved, The heart is blessed; It is in giving, not in seeking gifts, We find our quest. Whatever you longing for or may need, if you give; So shall your soul be fed, and thou indeed Shalt truly live. Cling to self, and you cling to sorrow, surrender self, and you enter into peace.

To seek selfishly is not only to lose happiness, but even that which we believe to be the source of happiness. See how the overeater is continually looking about for a new weakness to encourage his deadened appetite; and how, stuffed, loaded, and unhealthy, scarcely any food at last is eaten with pleasure. Whereas, he who has mastered his appetite, and not only does not seek, but never thinks of gustatory pleasure, finds delight in the most frugal meal. The angel-form of happiness, which men, looking through the eyes of self, imagine they see in gratified desire, when clasped is always found to be the skeleton of misery. Truly, "He that seeketh his life shall lose it, and he that loseth his life shall find it." Abiding happiness will come to you when, ceasing to selfishly cling, you are willing to give up.

When you are willing to lose, unreservedly, that impermanent thing which is so dear to you, and which, whether you cling to it or not, will one day be snatched from you, then you will find that that which seemed to you like a painful loss, turns out to be a supreme gain. To give up in order to gain, than this there is no greater delusion, nor no more prolific source of misery; but to be willing to yield up and to suffer loss, this is indeed the Way of Life. How is it possible to find real happiness by centering ourselves in those things which, by their very nature, must pass away? Abiding and real happiness can only be found by centering ourselves in that which is permanent. Rise, therefore, above the clinging to and the craving for impermanent things, and you will then enter into a consciousness of the Eternal, and as, rising above self, and by growing more and more into the spirit of purity, self-sacrifice and universal Love, you become centered in that consciousness, you will realize that happiness which has no reaction, and which can never be taken from you.

The heart that has reached utter self-forgetfulness in its love for others has not only become possessed of the highest happiness but has entered into immortality, for it has realized the Divine. Look back upon your life, and you will find that the moments of supremest happiness were those in which you uttered some word, or performed some act, of compassion or self-denying love. Spiritually, happiness and harmony are, synonymous. Harmony is one phase of the Great Law whose spiritual expression is love. All selfishness is discord, and to be selfish is to be out of harmony with the Divine order. As we realize that all-embracing love which is the negation of self, we put ourselves in harmony with the divine music, the universal song, and that ineffable melody which is true happiness becomes our own. Men and women are rushing hither and thither in the blind search for happiness, and cannot find it; nor ever will until they recognize that happiness is already within them and round about them, filling the universe, and that they, in their selfish searching are shutting themselves out from it. I followed happiness to make her mine, Past towering oak and swinging ivy vine. She fled, I chased, o'er slanting hill and dale, O'er fields and meadows, in the purpling vale; Pursuing rapidly o'er dashing stream. I scaled the dizzy cliffs where eagles scream; I traversed swiftly every land and M. But always happiness eluded me. Exhausted, fainting, I pursued no more, But sank to rest upon a barren shore. One came and asked for food, and one for alms I placed the bread and gold in bony palms. One came for sympathy, and one for rest; I shared with every needy one my best; When, Io! sweet Happiness, with form divine, Stood by me, whispering softly, 'I am thine'. These beautiful lines of Burleigh's express the secret of all abounding happiness. Sacrifice the personal and transient, and you rise at once into the impersonal and permanent. Give up that narrow cramped self that seeks to render all things subservient to its own petty interests, and you will enter into the company of the angels, into the very heart and essence of universal Love.

Forget yourself entirely in the sorrows of others and in ministering to others, and divine happiness will emancipate you from all sorrow and suffering. "Taking the first step with a good thought, the second with a good word, and the third with a good deed, I entered Paradise." And you also may enter into Paradise by pursuing the same course. It is not beyond, it is here. It is realized only by the unselfish. It is known in its fullness only to the pure in heart. If you have not realized this unbounded happiness you may begin to actualize it by ever holding before you the lofty ideal of unselfish love, and aspiring towards it. Aspiration or prayer is desire turned upward. It is the soul turning toward its Divine source, where alone permanent satisfaction can be found. aspiration the destructive forces of desire are transmuted into divine and all-preserving energy. To aspire is to make an effort to shake off the trammels of desire; it is the prodigal made wise by loneliness and suffering, returning to his Father's Mansion. As you rise above the sordid self; as you break, one after another, the chains that bind you, will you realize the joy of giving, as distinguished from the misery of grasping - giving of your substance; giving of your intellect;

giving of the love and light that is growing within you. You will then understand that it is indeed "more blessed to give than to receive." But the giving must be of the heart without any taint of self, without desire for reward. The gift of pure love is always attended with bliss. If, after you have given, you are wounded because you are not thanked or flattered, or your name put in the paper, know then that your gift was prompted by vanity and not by love, and you were merely giving in order to get; were not really giving, but grasping. Lose yourself in the welfare of others; forget yourself in all that you do; this is the secret of abounding happiness.

Ever be on the watch to guard against selfishness, and learn faithfully the divine lessons of inward sacrifice; so shall you climb the highest heights of happiness, and shall remain in the neverclouded sunshine of universal joy, clothed in the shining garment of immortality. Are you searching for the happiness that does not fade away? Are you looking for the joy that lives, and leaves no grievous day? Are you panting for the waterbrooks of Love, and Life, and Peace? Then let all dark desires depart, and selfish seeking cease. Are you ling'ring in the paths of pain, grief-haunted, stricken sore? Are you wand'ring in the ways that wound your weary feet the more? Are you sighing for the Resting-Place where tears and sorrows cease? Then sacrifice your selfish heart and find the Heart of Peace.

THE INSIGHT OF PROSPERITY

2 CORINTHIANS 1:20 For all the promises of God in Him are Yes, and in Him Amen, to the glory of God through us.

GALATIANS 3:14 that the blessing of Abraham might come upon the Gentiles in Christ Jesus, that we might receive the promise of the Spirit through faith.

GALATIANS 3:16 Now to Abraham and his Seed were the promises made. He does not say, "And to seeds," as of many, but as of one, "And to your Seed," who is Christ.

HEBREWS 10:1 For the law, having a shadow of the good things to come, and not the very image....

GALATIANS 2:6 But from those who seemed to be something-- whatever they were, it makes no difference to me; God shows personal favoritism to no man....

ACTS 10:34 Then Peter opened his mouth and said: "In truth I perceive that God shows no partiality. ROMANS 2:11 For there is no partiality with God.

GENESIS 1:28 Then God blessed them, and God said to them, "Be fruitful and multiply; fill the earth and subdue it; have dominion over the fish of the sea, over the birds of the air, and over every living thing that moves on the earth."

GENESIS 9:1 So God blessed Noah and his sons, and said to them: "Be fruitful and multiply, and fill the earth. GENESIS 9:7

And as for you, be fruitful and multiply; bring forth abundantly in the earth and multiply in it."

GENESIS 12:2 I will make you a great nation; I will bless you and make your name great; and you shall be a blessing.

GENESIS 13:2 Abram was very rich in livestock, in silver, and in gold.

GENESIS 24:1 Now Abraham was old, well-advanced in age; and the Lord had blessed Abraham in all things.

GENESIS 24:35 "The Lord has blessed my master greatly, and he has become great; and He has given him flocks and herds, silver and gold, male and female servants, and camels and donkeys.

GENESIS 26:12 Then Isaac sowed in that land, and reaped in the same year a hundredfold; and the Lord blessed him.

THE INSIGHT OF PROSPERITY It is granted only to the heart that abounds with integrity, trust, generosity and love to realize true prosperity. The heart that is not possessed of these qualities cannot know prosperity, for prosperity, like happiness, is not an outward possession, but an inward realization. The greedy man may become a millionaire, but he will always be worthless, and mean, and poor, and will even consider himself outwardly poor so long as there is a man/woman in the world who is richer than himself/herself, though the upright, the open-handed and loving will realize a full and rich prosperity, even though their outward possessions may be small. He is poor who is dissatisfied; he is rich who is contented with what he has, and he is richer who is generous with what he has. When we contemplate the fact that the universe is abounding in all good things, material as well as spiritual, and compare it with man's blind eagerness to secure a few gold coins, or a few acres of dirt, it is then that we realize how dark and ignorant selfishness is; it is then that we know that self-seeking is self-destruction. Nature gives all, without reservation, and loses nothing; man, grasping all, loses everything. If you would realize true prosperity do not settle down, as many have done, into the belief that if you do right everything will go wrong. Do not allow the word "competition" to shake your faith in the supremacy of righteousness.

I care not what men may say about the "laws of competition," while I focus on what mates and for I do not know the unchangeable Law, which shall one day put them all to rout, and which puts them to rout even now in the heart and life of the righteous man? And knowing this Law I can contemplate all dishonesty with undisturbed repose, for I know where certain destruction awaits it. Under all circumstances do that which you believe to be right, and trust the Law; trust the Divine Power that is imminent in the universe, and it will never desert you, and you will always be protected. By such a trust all your losses will be converted into gains, and all curses which threaten will be transmuted into blessings. Never let go of integrity, generosity, and love, for these, coupled with energy, will lift you into the truly prosperous state. Do not believe the world when it tells you that you must always attend to "number one" first, and to others afterwards. To do this is not to think of others at all, but only of one's own comforts. To those who practice this the day will come when they will be deserted by all, and when they cry out in their loneliness and anguish there will be no one to hear and help them. To consider one's self before all others is to cramp and warp and hinder every noble and divine impulse. Let your soul expand, let your heart reach out to others in loving and generous warmth, and great and lasting will be your joy, and all prosperity will come to you.

Those who have wandered from the highway of righteousness guard themselves against competition; those who always pursue the right need not to trouble about such defense. This is no empty statement, There are men today who, by the power of integrity and faith, have defied all competition, and who, without swerving in the least from their methods, when competed with, have risen steadily into prosperity, whilst those who tried to undermine them have fallen back defeated. To possess those inward qualities which constitute goodness is to be armored against all the powers of evil, and to be doubly protected in every time of trial; and to build' oneself up in those qualities is to build up a success which cannot be shaken, and to enter into a prosperity which will endure forever. The White Robe of the Heart Invisible Is stained with sin and sorrow, grief and pain, And all repentant pools and springs of prayer Shall not avail to wash it white again.

While in the path of ignorance I walk, The stains of error will not cease to cling Defilements mark the crooked path of self, Where anguish lurks and disappointments sting. Knowledge and wisdom only can avail To purify and make my garment clean, For therein lie love's waters ; therein rests Peace undisturbed, eternal, and serene. Sin and repentance is the path of pain, Knowledge and wisdom is the path of Peace By the near way of practice I will find Where bliss begins, how pains and sorrows cease. Self shall depart, and Truth shall take its place The Changeless One, the Indivisible Shall take up His abode in me, and cleanse The White Robe of the Heart Invisible.

To Be Rich

GENESIS 26:13 The man began to prosper, and continued prospering until he became very prosperous;

GENESIS 26:14 for he had possessions of flocks and possessions of herds and a great number of servants. So the Philistines envied him.

GENESIS 30:43 Thus the man became exceedingly prosperous, and had large flocks, female and male servants, and camels and donkeys.

GENESIS 39:2 The Lord was with Joseph, and he was a successful man; and he was in the house of his master the Egyptian.

GENESIS 39:3 And his master saw that the Lord was with him and that the Lord made all he did to prosper in his hand.

GENESIS 39:5 So it was, from the time that he had made him overseer of his house and all that he had, that the Lord blessed the Egyptian's house for Joseph's sake; and the blessing of the Lord was on all that he had in the house and in the field.

GENESIS 39:23 The keeper of the prison did not look into anything that was under Joseph's hand, because the Lord was with him; and whatever he did, the Lord made it prosper.

EXODUS 19:5 'Now therefore, if you will indeed obey My voice and keep My covenant, then you shall be a special treasure to Me above all people; for all the earth is Mine.

LEVITICUS 25:21 'Then I will command My blessing on you in the sixth year, and it will bring forth produce enough for three years.

LEVITICUS 25:23 'The land shall not be sold permanently, for the land is Mine; for you are strangers and sojourners with Me.

LEVITICUS 26:9 For I will look on you favorably and make you fruitful, multiply you and confirm My covenant with you.

DEUTERONOMY 2:7 "For the Lord your God has blessed you in all the work of your hand. He knows your trudging through this great wilderness. These forty years the Lord your God has been with you; you have lacked nothing.'"

DEUTERONOMY 7:13 "And He will love you and bless you and multiply you; He will also bless the fruit of your womb and the fruit of your land, your grain and your new wine and your oil, the increase of your cattle and the offspring of your flock, in the land of which He swore to your fathers to give you.

DEUTERONOMY 8:9 "a land in which you will eat bread without scarcity, in which you will lack nothing; a land whose stones are iron and out of whose hills you can dig copper.

Jacob was a man not without faith in God. The Bible speaks of the God of Abraham, Isaac and Jacob. But as we observe the events of his early career, it appears that in marked contrast to Abraham, it was Jacob's desire, more than anything else in the world, to become rich. Jacob had observed how God had prospered his grandfather and he saw and coveted this prosperity. But apparently he knew little or nothing of that supreme consecration that Abraham had made to Jehovah which was the basis of his prosperity. He had little opportunity to cultivate the acquaintance of his grandfather, for he died while

Jacob was yet a lad of fifteen. The youth, not knowing the secrets of Abraham's wealth, was fired with an ambition to attain his outward prosperity. In his way of thinking there was one way to secure it, and that was "to get all he could while the getting was good." At the same time he would be a worshipper of Jehovah. He would show that it was possible to serve both God and mammon!

THE BIRTHRIGHT AND THE BLESSING (Gen. 25-28)

According to custom, the birthright belonged to the eldest son. Jacob and Esau were twins, but Esau was born first, therefore the birthright was his. Jacob considered this a great misfortune, and he began to consider ways and means by which he might get it transferred into his own possession. He decided that the way to accomplish his objective was to wait until Esau was in a desperate plight. He knew his brother loved to hunt and would rather spend his time in that occupation than anything else. But hunting was profitable only when the seasons were favorable. Sometimes there were drouths and the game would retreat to remote parts.

Esau did not like farming and had no income from the field to fall back upon. At such a time Jacob foresaw he might be able to drive a hard bargain. He bided his time, and the day came when Esau returned from the field faint and emptyhanded and was—so he thought—about to perish from hunger. Jacob was now ready to make a bargain with him, but only if he would trade him his birthright. In a moment of weakness the bargain was made, which Esau was to regret the rest of his life. But Jacob was not yet satisfied. He knew that his father, Isaac, intended to bestow a special blessing upon Esau, his elder and favorite son. He coveted that blessing for himself. There was more scheming and planning. With the connivance of his mother, Rebekah, who had some good qualities, yet also seemed to possess a streak of intrigue, the two schemed to get the blessing for Jacob, in addition to the birthright he had already secured. To them the end seemed to justify the means. When Isaac spoke to his son, Esau, that the time had come to give him the blessing, and while his son went out into the fields to secure savoury meat for him, Jacob and his mother set their plan into operation. A couple of young goats were killed to make a savoury meat. The skins of the kids were put on Jacob's hands and neck to simulate the feel of the skin of Esau. Thus Isaac, deceived as to the identity of the one before him, gave the blessing to Jacob. But that was far from the end of the story, as we shall see. Jacob was to pay over and over for his deception. He was forced to leave home. Never again was he to see his mother, Rebekah. His hopes of enjoying the inheritance he had secured by trickery were soon dispelled. He was forced to flee for his life from his enraged brother, Esau. With only what he would carry with him, he made the long journey to his mother's people in far-off Padan- Aram.

SCHEMING IN PADAN-ARAM (Gen. 29-31)

Here in the land of the East, Jacob made his home. Though he had received an experience with God at Bethel, he had not yet given up his shrewd practices. But here he met people who were just as shrewd as he was. He worked in Padan-Aram seven years to secure the wife he loved, but at the end of the time, he found that Laban had craftily interjected a condition into the contract. Pleading the customs of the land, Laban told Jacob that the younger daughter could not be given before the elder (Gen. 29:26). So it was that he had an unwanted wife on his hands, and had to work another seven years to get the one he loved. It was a battle of wits of one trader against another. Jacob apparently had met his match. Laban shortchanged Jacob again and again. Jacob complained to his wives that their father had changed his wages ten times (Gen. 31:7). In the end, however, Jacob's cunning outwitted the maneuverings of his father-inlaw. In connection with an arrangement with Laban, Jacob's discovery of certain biological laws enabled him to secure possession of the stronger of the cattle. In so doing he incurred

pg. 49

the animosity of Laban's sons. The time came when Jacob saw that there was mischief on foot against him. He would do as he had done before when trouble came: he would flee. But this time he would see that everything he had secured claim to would be taken with him. And that is when Jacob's troubles really began. Laban came after him, intending to avenge himself of his troublesome son-in-law. However he was restrained from this, due to divine intervention (Gen. 31:29). Having escaped the danger from the rear, tidings came to Jacob of still graver dangers ahead. He had dared to hope that Esau, by this time, had forgotten the old feud. Apparently he was wrong. The news reached him that Esau was coming against him with 400 men of war (Gen. 32:6). Jacob was alarmed. He realized the signs indicated that his brother was not coming in peace. Not if he was coming to meet him with an army of 400! What should he do? Jacob at last came face to face with reality. There was no running from danger now, for there was no way to run. He had only one last recourse and that was God.

THE CHANGE (Gen. 32)

That night, Jacob went across the brook Jabbok and was left alone. There he wrestled with the angel of God. In the distance he knew that Esau was coming to execute vengeance. No one but God could help him. But in that night of travail a new man was born—Israel, a prince with God! That night Jacob was to learn that there were other things more important than the material things of this world that could so easily be taken from him. For the first time he saw that spiritual things must rank first. God will give His people material blessings, but first they must seek the spiritual. As Jesus said, "Seek ye first the kingdom of God, and his righteousness; and all these things shall be added unto you" (Matt. 6:33). Jacob won a notable victory that night. He had prevailed with God. When Esau appeared on the scene he was a changed man. Instead of a bloody battle, the two brothers melted into each other's arms. Jacob, instead of scheming to outwit his brother by driving a sharp bargain, wanted to divide his herd with Esau. And Esau, instead of eagerly accepting the gift, had to be urged to accept. But Jacob had not yet paid the full price of his evil sowing. Years of misdeeds are not expiated in a moment. The foundations of prosperity have to be laid. It was many years before Jacob would have the peace his heart longed for. True, he had the peace that comes from being a believer in Jehovah. But his sons had not learned their lesson. They, like he once was, were carnal, envious, grasping, and even murderous. His favorite wife, Rachel, was a devotee of image worship. Jacob apparently got her to give up her gods and turn to Jehovah (Gen. 35:1-4). But not long after, she died during the birth of their son, Benjamin. Many other misfortunes befell him. Dinah, his daughter, was violated. Simeon and Levi went on a murderous rampage, taking the lives of many innocent people in a mission to avenge their sister. Reuben committed incest with one of his father's wives. The other sons broke their father's heart by their treacherous conduct in selling their brother, Joseph, into Egypt. Jacob had once deceived his father, Isaac, by killing a kid and using its skin to deceive Jacob. "Whatsoever a man soweth, that shall he also reap" (Gal. 6:7) is an eternal principle that none may ignore with impunity. However, there came the time when things changed and the last years of Jacob's life were good years.

When the change came, it took place suddenly. In the midst of distresses occasioned by the severe famine, came the strange tidings that his son, Joseph, long thought dead, was indeed alive and had been made lord over all the land of Egypt. This was his message to the family of Jacob: "Now thou art commanded, this do ye; take you wagons out of the land of Egypt for your little ones, and for your wives, and bring your father, and come. Also regard not your stuff; for the good of all the land of Egypt is yours" (Gen. 45:19,20). Jacob was thus commanded to leave all and come at once to Joseph. All that he could desire in the way of temporal blessings was now his. Jacob had learned his lesson. God gives wealth to His children who will use it for His glory. He may withhold it from those who desperately seek it, or who will not use it for His glory. Material blessings are for believers who seek first the kingdom of God.

Write down What you have you Learned from this Teaching & Reading?

1

2

3

4

5

Books by the Author

Sheka Mansaray

1. The Tears of My Father: My Gift to the World

2. DESERT ROSE: WORDS FOR THOUGHTS

3. Warfare Time: (Spiritual Warfare)

4. Carrier of Christ's Light: (Arise, shine, for your light has come)

5. Revelation Today (Living A life of Faith Daily Vol)

6. Unveiling Prosperity INSIGHT OF PROSPERITY Vol 1

Author Biography

Sheka Mansaray is the founder and Pastor of "Faith Embassy International Ministries" a multi-cultural, non-denominational church. Mansaray is the founder of Sheka Mansaray Ministries, a partnership-based outreach ministry with a solid Apostolic and Prophetic Mandate. Mansaray is also the founder of "Alpha Business Network" a network of current and future business owners. He is a gifted Poet, Writer, Philanthropist, Entrepreneur, and Author. Sheka Mansaray is a husband, happily married to his wife, Nanah Mansaray; and a father to their two children, daughter, Faith Mansaray; and Son, Sheka Jeremiah Mansaray Jr.

www.ingramcontent.com/pod-product-compliance
Lightning Source LLC
Chambersburg PA
CBHW071124210326
41519CB00020B/6414